HE'S THE GOD

OF A

Second

Chance!

by RICHARD ROBERTS

*Unless otherwise indicated,
all Scripture quotations
are from the King James Version
of the Bible.*

Table of Contents

He's the God of a Second Chance

People often say to me, "Richard Roberts, you're different than I am. You don't have problems in your life like I do — you're famous! You couldn't possibly know the kinds of heartache that ordinary people face."

And I wonder why anyone would think that being well known somehow makes you exempt from pain...from failure...or from gut-wrenching heartache in your life.

That's one reason why I decided to write this book. Yes, I've lived in the "limelight" most of my life. But one thing I can say about it from my own experience is this: when it comes down to the nuts and bolts of life, I'm no different than you are. I know what it is to hurt.

Several years ago I went through an experience that is one of the hardest experiences any human being can face — a divorce. I *know* the heartache of that time. I know what it is to be down and to wonder if you'll ever get up again...to fail just about as miserably as a man *can* fail. I've been there.

But through all of my struggles, I've learned one immovable fact that I can stake my life on... *the God I serve is the God of a SECOND CHANCE!* He's not a God of judgment or punishment or vengeance, just waiting to slap us down when we make a mistake. He's a loving, forgiving, miracle-working God who can take our worst sins and our deepest sorrows and *turn those things around for our good.*

If He is not the God of a SECOND CHANCE, then how do you explain Richard Roberts? How do you explain my life and the healing ministry God has given me? In many people's eyes, I above all people should have been thrown out with the garbage. But when I realized what I'd done with my life and got down on my knees and told God I was sorry, God turned my problems around.

I may never have been in the healing ministry I'm in today, of preaching the gospel and praying for the sick, if God were not the God of a SECOND CHANCE. It was only after my greatest failures and defeats that God has brought about some of my greatest victories in Him.

Friend, we *all* make mistakes and fail. (See Romans 3:23.) You'll never find anyone who doesn't. But when you give those failures to Jesus, you don't have to be ashamed anymore. You can stand up straight with your shoulders back and say, "God, are You finished with me? Or do You have something more You want me to do?" And you can start over again . . . just like I did. And when you *do,* I guarantee you'll find out, just like the words to a song I sing, that "God's not through blessing *you.*"

RR

I.

A Dream Is Born

*Have you ever tried growing up as Oral Roberts'
son? If you haven't, you ought to try it sometime.*
That's what I always tell people when they start
to bring up the subject of my growing-up years. So
far, I've never had any "takers."

Actually, growing up as Oral Roberts' son was
very interesting. It had its bad times, that's true.
But it also had its good times, especially when my
dad was able to be home with us for several days
at a time between crusades. At times like that in
my life, I would have paid all the money in the
world to be Oral Roberts' son. But there were other
times when I wouldn't have given you a plug nickel
for it.

Dad traveled on the road, conducting great tent
crusades in this country and around the world,
most of my childhood. In fact, my mother said that
he was often gone from home three weeks out of
four. Sometimes as a child that was hard to accept.

I remember one time when I was about six or
seven years old, Dad was getting ready to leave
for Australia to conduct a crusade. It was bad

enough that he had to be gone for six weeks, but to make matters worse, he had the nerve to plan to take Mother with him! That was almost too much for me and my little sister, Roberta, to bear. We threw a hissy-fit to try to keep them from leaving. I remember it very well. They had just given me a little hatchet for my birthday. And I took that hatchet and chopped one of the knobs off the end of my bed, hoping they would change their minds and stay home. Of course, it didn't work. I can still remember hearing my dad's words, "I have no choice about going, Richard. If I had a choice, I wouldn't go; I'd stay home with my children. But I must go and obey God."

Imagine being six or seven years old and trying to understand those words. I couldn't . . . because I didn't yet understand what having the call of God on your life meant. I just knew that my dad and mother were leaving us for six weeks.

In the summertime when school was out, Mother often took us with her to Dad's crusades. We all loved to sit on the front row! We'd listen to my dad preach and watch him pray for the sick as they came through the healing lines, just waiting for the miracles to happen. You never knew when someone would jump up out of a wheelchair or when deaf ears would be opened or blind eyes would be healed. And when it happened, the entire crowd got so excited they'd almost go right up through the top of the tent!

I gave my heart to Jesus as a seven-year-old boy in one of those crusades. I remember it vividly. In fact, when I close my eyes and think of those crusades, I can almost smell the sawdust.

I fell in love with the healing ministry of Jesus Christ by watching my dad and I began to dream of having a healing ministry of my own someday. It was a secret dream deep in my heart that no one else knew anything about. It lodged in my soul and stayed there all my growing-up years. In the back of my mind, even when I later ran away from God as a teenager, I wondered what God would have for my life someday.

Dad and I were very close in my childhood days. He loved sports and he taught me how to hunt and fish, how to play baseball, tennis, and golf. In fact, I often tell people that Dad put a golf club in my hands when I was just five years old! Many people remember me only as a skinny little boy with a fishing pole in one hand and a baseball glove in the other.

Yes, there were some wonderful times growing up as the son of an internationally known healing evangelist, but there were some really tough times too. I remember the times when the other children in school — and sometimes even the teachers — would make fun of me. It wasn't unusual for a group of kids to run up to me, put their hands on my forehead and scream "Heal!" in imitation of my dad praying for the sick, and then run away laughing.

I came home from school many a day with my shirt torn and my nose bloodied from being in fights with the other kids who made fun of me, my dad, and the healing ministry of Jesus Christ. I even wondered *myself* if I'd ever amount to anything.

I also read what the newspapers had to say about "that shyster" Oral Roberts. Times like that drove me inside myself. It hurt me and it made me angry that they would say and do the things they did because that was my *dad* they were talking about. He was the man I loved. He was the man who came home to us dead tired from weeks on the road of preaching the gospel and praying for the sick, and yet he made time... real quality time... for us during the few days he could be home.

The older I got, the more I saw how other people felt about the healing ministry that my dad was so involved in. The more I saw, the more I hurt. And the more I hurt, the more I withdrew from my dad, from the healing ministry, and from God. Living my life to please God or my parents soon became the farthest thing from my mind. For years I put God on a shelf. I literally ran away from the healing call of God on my life.

And if God were not the God of a Second Chance, perhaps I would have succeeded during those years in shutting out the dream that God had placed in my heart of one day serving Him in a healing ministry of my own.

What About You?

Do you have a dream in your heart that has almost died because something or someone you love has hurt you? Have you allowed bitterness to come into your heart? Maybe it's a dream you've just had for a few months or a few years... or

maybe it's one you've had in your heart from your
earliest memories. Maybe it's a dream like mine
that I hardly dared believe could ever happen to
me...and yet with all my heart I wanted that
dream to become reality.

I believe that God places a dream in all of our
hearts of what *He* has for our life someday if we'll
only follow Him and trust Him to bring it into
reality...no matter what the circumstances of our
life look like...no matter who or what has hurt
us...no matter how many times we get knocked
down and our dream seems to shatter to pieces
right in front of our eyes.

Maybe you feel like you'll fail before you can
ever begin because someone said to you as a child,
"Well, *he'll* never amount to anything" or *"She'll*
never do anything for God in her life." My friend,
I know how that feels.

But, praise God! The God I serve is the GOD OF
A SECOND CHANCE! He specializes in mending
broken dreams...in healing wounded hearts...
and in making something beautiful out of our lives.

I pray that as you read the rest of this book,
you'll see how the hopes and dreams you thought
were long since buried in the ashes of your mistakes
and failures can be resurrected in your heart to live
again. Because when you turn your life over to the
GOD OF A SECOND CHANCE, He'll take the
broken pieces of your dream. He'll give you back a
plan for your life more wonderful than you ever
dreamed possible.

Yes...if He can do it for Richard Roberts, He
can do it for you.

II.

Singing Becomes My Life

All my life I've loved to sing. In fact, when I was just five years old, my dad stood me up on a chair in front of his crusade crowd in Baltimore, Maryland. I made my public singing debut with "I Believe." As a teenager I continued to sing, but not in my dad's crusades. I had decided by then that I didn't have time for God in my life. And I found that I had less and less time for my family too.

I began to get involved in all kinds of musical productions, plays, operas, and operettas, at school and other places. I learned to play the guitar and began singing in pizza parlors around Tulsa where I lived. Then I moved on into the nightclub circuit in town and around the state of Oklahoma.

A different dream began to come into my heart. It was not the dream God had given me of one day praying for the sick. It was a new dream of becoming a nightclub singer in Las Vegas. I began to gear my life toward being a professional singer in the one place in this country that signaled "success" in the eyes of the world.

There was no doubt in my mind that I had the

talent to do it. Many people, including professional talent scouts, told me that I did. As I moved my life in that direction, I soon became the lead singer in a very successful rock band, traveling each weekend to cities throughout the state playing the guitar and singing.

I was on my way to success! I just didn't have time for anything else. I didn't realize it but I was headed on a collision course.

During a vacation from school I went with my mother to Dad's crusade in Daytona Beach, Florida. It so happened that one of my dad's associates had been talking to Dad about my singing.

My dad had known about my love for singing but had never said much about it, at least not to me. We were in his hotel room one afternoon before the service that night, and Dad brought up the subject of singing.

He said, "Richard, I've noticed how much singing you've been doing at school and other places and I wondered if you would sing for me in the service tonight?"

It was a simple enough request, one that I would have been happy to oblige a few years before. But this time something came over me. I looked him straight in the eye and I said, "No, Dad, I won't."

"Why not?" he asked.

"I just don't want to," was my reply.

"Well, Richard, you have such a good voice, I'm sure everyone would like to hear you."

"Dad, I'm just not interested in singing tonight."

"O.K., Richard, I understand. But do you have something against . . . "

"No, I'm just...just leave me alone," I said with finality in my voice.

That ended the discussion for that night. But the next night he started on me again.

"Richard, will you sing tonight?"

"No, Dad, I don't want to."

And so it went the next night...and the next night...

"Richard, will you sing *tonight*?"

"No, Dad, I don't want to."

He'd ask and I'd say no. He'd ask and I'd say no. Gradually a wall began to be built between my dad and me. He'd push and I'd push back. He'd push more and I'd push back more. I didn't want him asking me to sing in his crusades and I didn't want him pressuring me about my relationship with Jesus Christ. Actually I had *no* active relationship with Jesus at that time. It had fallen by the wayside as I pursued my goal of singing. I knew I couldn't talk about a relationship that I didn't have. So the wall kept getting higher. Finally there was nothing left to say.

During my senior year in high school I applied at three different out-of-state universities. I was accepted at all three. This was a great relief because Oral Roberts University had just opened the year before. And the last place in the world I wanted to go to school was Oral Roberts University! I mean, who wants to go to college where your dad's the president? Certainly not *me*!

All during high school, I had taken some pretty rough abuse because of my dad's ministry. I'd had a lot of criticism thrown at me about him and his healing ministry and I was sick and tired of it.

Can you understand how I felt... the paradox I was in?

On the one hand, I just wanted to be rid of the whole thing because it was too painful to bear. But on the other hand, this was my dad they were talking about. I think I had the same instinct that any child would have, to defend something or someone he loved.

So against my parents' wishes, I left Oklahoma and enrolled in a state university. I let it be known I didn't want to be anywhere near the school my father was building. But the real reason I didn't want to go to ORU was because I didn't want to have God jammed down my throat.

It worked... for a while. No one talked to me about God or about singing for Jesus. I got to live in a co-ed dorm. I got to wear anything I wanted to wear and do anything I wanted to do. I went to bed when I wanted to and got up when I wanted to. If I didn't want to go to class, I didn't have to. All I had to do was show up for the tests. It made no difference to anyone what I had had to drink or had put in my system the night before.

I felt I was having the time of my life!

Then I went home to Tulsa for semester break. It was wintertime and cold. But one day the weather changed and it warmed up to springtime temperatures. Dad and I decided to go out and play nine holes of golf together.

We went out to the golf course and were having the greatest time. It was just like the times I remembered as a little boy when Dad and I were

together. But on the sixth green as I was standing
over a putt, he ruined everything. I'll never forget
what happened . . .

"Richard, I'm having a seminar on campus tonight," Dad said. "There will be hundreds of people
there. Would you just come and sing one song?"

Suddenly that old fire began rising up on the
inside of me. It was as if I had my fists doubled
up and wanted to hit somebody. I looked at him
with as much fire as I could muster coming out of
my eyes and snarled, "Look, Dad, just get off my
back and get out of my life. And don't you ever
mention God to me again."

And those were among the nicer things I said!
But, you know, my dad really surprised me that
day. He said, "All right, Richard, I'll never mention
God to you again unless you ask me to."

"Fine," I shot back. And suddenly the game
ended. I left the golf course, got back in my car,
and as fast as I could arrange it, I left Tulsa and
drove to college for the second semester. I thought,
Well, that settles that once and for all, because I
knew my dad was a man of his word. If he said
he wouldn't mention God to me again unless I
asked him, I knew he wouldn't do it.

I think that probably was the greatest favor my
dad ever did for me . . . and I mean that in the right
way. Because when he quit talking to me about
God, I quit having to listen to a man's voice and
I began hearing another Voice instead. At the time
I didn't know who that Voice was, but I knew I
was hearing and feeling something different on
the inside of me. It wasn't something I could

describe to anyone else, but it was there.

I really believed that as soon as I got back to school everything would be fine. But what I didn't know was that my world would begin falling apart right in front of my eyes.

Immediately I got sick and had to be hospitalized with a bad colon infection. Someone said to me, "Well, God *caused* you to be sick." But I knew that to be a lie because I knew sickness wasn't from God. Even though I didn't really have a relationship with God then and certainly wasn't living a life to honor Him, I had been raised in church and on the Bible. I knew that God is a good God and He never makes people sick; sickness is an oppression of the devil. (See Acts 10:38.)

And even though I wasn't living out those beliefs, somewhere in my heart I still knew they were true. The Bible says, "Train up a child in the way he should go: and when he is old, he will not depart from it" (Proverbs 22:6). That's what my parents had done.

One thing did happen to me, though, while I was sick. For the first time in several years I began thinking about God! It's amazing, isn't it, that when you get sick God seems to come across your mind? Have you ever noticed that? Sometimes people go for years without thinking about Him until they get sick or in some other kind of jam. Then it all comes back to them.

Well, out of my sickness and pain came one of the greatest experiences I've ever had. For the first time in my life I discovered that our God is the GOD OF A SECOND CHANCE. That discovery began to turn my life around.

What About You?

Have you ever gotten on the wrong path in your life? Have you ever made a decision to go one way with your life when deep down in your heart you knew you were supposed to go another?

Or maybe you've been caught in a relationship with someone like I was with my dad. You love that other person but somehow they just seem to ask you too many questions about your life and your relationship with the Lord. And you don't know how to answer their questions because, like me, you can't talk about a relationship you don't have.

My friend, when you choose to leave God out of your life — whether it's a willful decision like mine was or just because you never seem to have time to think about Him — you're making the greatest mistake of your life. Everything may appear to be going smoothly right now, but I believe the day will come when your back's against the wall just like mine was. The Bible says that sin is only pleasurable for a season (see Hebrews 11:25) and then it begins to tear you apart. And you'd be surprised how important God can suddenly become to you when that happens.

But the good news is that God can forgive you of your sin and turn your life around ... if you'll only ask Him. (See 1 John 1:9.)

You say, "Richard Roberts, is it really possible

for me to get my life back on track and have a personal relationship with God, even though I've turned my back on Him all these years?"

Yes, it is, my friend. He's the GOD OF A SECOND CHANCE for *you.*

III.

From the Wrong Place to the Right Place ... and Jesus

While I was sick in the hospital I had a lot of time to think. And I began thinking about all *kinds* of things. I thought I had friends there at that university, but when I got sick they all deserted me. Suddenly I realized that I was all alone. I felt like I was just a number, one of thousands of students. And I found out what being really lonely feels like.

Even before going into the hospital, I'd had to drop several classes because of my sickness. And afterward I couldn't attend any classes while I was recuperating. One day after I checked out of the hospital and was back in my dormitory room, I heard a Voice.

You're in the wrong place, the Voice said.

I looked around ... and strangely enough, there was no one in the room with me! I opened the closet door, went over and looked under the bed, and *still* there was no one there.

But I was determined to find out where that Voice was coming from! So I looked out the window to see if someone was hanging on the outside of the building . . . and suddenly the Voice spoke again.

You're in the wrong place.

Well, that made me angry. And I said back, "What do you mean I'm in the wrong place? Who are you?"

I didn't know then like I know now that it was the Holy Spirit speaking to my heart. I just knew that I heard a Voice . . . saying something I didn't want to hear. Some people may think that sounds crazy. But there *was* a Voice speaking *inside* of me somewhere and I heard it. And I've got good hearing!

You're at the wrong university, the Voice said this time.

"What do you mean I'm at the wrong university?" I asked. And then I asked a question that was the dumbest question I could ever have asked for someone who wanted to live his life *his* way and leave God out of the picture.

I asked, "What university should I be at?"

And guess what the Voice said? *You're supposed to be at Oral Roberts University.*

Ohhh . . . did I blow it that time! *That* was the last thing I ever wanted to hear. Day after day and week after week throughout that second semester I kept hearing that Voice say the same thing and it wouldn't let me go.

Sometimes people laugh when I tell that because it sounds so strange. *But I believe that's how the Holy Spirit deals with you.* I not only believe it, I *know* it because that's how He dealt with me. He keeps speaking to your heart and speaking to your heart about what you should do and He doesn't let go of you just because you say no one time.

So finally one day I stopped fighting and resisting the Spirit. I said, "All right, all right. I'll call ORU and see if they'll accept me." But before I called ORU I called my parents to ask their opinion. *Their* opinion? My, I was changing already! My mother said, "Richard, I don't know if they will accept you because of your habits. You can't smoke and drink and do other things like that and be an ORU student. Besides that," she said, "they may already be full for next year."

"But, Mother," I said, "I can change. I can give up those habits."

After we finished talking I called the Oral Roberts University Director of Admissions. I said to him, "I know all the applications are probably in for next semester and you probably don't have room for me, but I'd like to come back to ORU ..."

Before I could even finish my sentence, he cut in, "Richard, we'll *make* a spot for you. You just come on." I guess they had more faith in me than I had in myself.

Well, now I'd really done it.

I finished out the rest of that year at the state university, then spent the summer working as a singer/actor at the Kansas City Starlight Theater. In September I moved back home and enrolled at ORU. And, believe me, it was one of the most difficult things I'd ever done in my life!

Overnight, I had to learn how to wear a shirt and tie to class. I had to learn how to *go* to class again ... and to the twice-weekly chapel services that are required when you're a student at Oral Roberts University. I had to sign an Honor Code, pledging that I would keep all the rules and regulations of ORU.

Boy, what a drag, I thought, but those were the rules, so I went along with them like everyone else. Before long I began to realize that the only thing that had *changed* about me was my physical proximity from that other university to Tulsa . . . nothing else had really changed! I was still the same person with the same dream of someday becoming a nightclub singer in Las Vegas.

I hadn't been at Oral Roberts University very long when both the Dean of Men *and* the Dean of Women had to call me in to discuss my "habits" that were different from most of the other students on campus. I hadn't given up either smoking or drinking. And I'd gotten involved in many other things at the other university that I was still doing. Except at ORU it was a little more obvious. You know, when you walk into your dorm room and you've been smoking, it's pretty easy to tell if you're the only one in the whole dormitory who smokes!

And then, to make matters worse, one day I heard a rumor about me. I heard that from the moment I'd walked on the ORU campus, prayer groups had been praying for me.

Now that made me angry.

It was one thing for *me* to do what that Voice had told me to do, but it was another thing altogether for these *other people* to get involved in it . . . to be praying for me to get saved! I thought, *The nerve of those other students. Why don't they just leave me alone!*

I'd walk down the hallway in my dorm and hear

a group of people praying in one of the rooms. And
if I put my ear to the door, sometimes I'd hear my
name being called out to God in prayer.

And that *really* hacked me off! I didn't want
those people praying for me or getting involved in
my life in any way . . . *until* it finally started to get
to me after several weeks. Because, you know, when
you have a group of people praying for you, who
really care for you and you know it, somehow it
gets down on the inside of you.

People would come up to me on campus or sometimes in the dorm and put their arm around me.
They'd give me a pat on the back and say they
cared about me . . . and I knew they really did. I
could feel that they did and I liked that. And I
found out something very important. I found out
that my heart wasn't as "cold as stone" as I thought
it was. I wanted those people to care about me. No
one at that other university had ever done those
things. I was just a number . . . one of 17,000 students who came in and punched the little ticket
at the first of each semester. No one really knew
me there.

So the way everyone at ORU treated me and
cared about me really began to get to me.

One Sunday afternoon I went home to talk to
my parents about what was on my mind . . . about
how miserable I had been feeling about my life.
Dad was out of town conducting a crusade in Los
Angeles. But my mother was there. I began to
pour my heart out to her like I hadn't done in many,
many years. She put her arms around me and
listened to how I felt, and then she said, "Richard,

you're never going to be happy and fulfilled until you have a personal relationship with Jesus Christ."

And suddenly I knew exactly what she meant! I'd never really had a personal relationship with Jesus since I was old enough to make a real commitment of my life to Him. I knew I had to do it that day.

So at the age of 19 — just two weeks before my twentieth birthday — I put my head in my mother's lap like I'd done so many times as a little boy and I repeated a very simple sinner's prayer after her. And when I'd finished confessing my sins and asking God to forgive me, *I felt for the first time in my life that I could make it.*

In that one moment, my life was completely transformed. The dream I'd had of becoming a nightclub singer in Las Vegas suddenly vanished. A new dream and a new desire to serve God came into my heart. Actually it was a very old dream — but it hadn't been there for a long time.

Oh, sure, I'd stood to accept Jesus as a little seven-year-old boy, but through the years that decision had faded away. Now...Jesus was becoming a *real Person* to me. Jesus wasn't just someone in the Bible, someone who had lived 2,000 years before. He was a living, breathing Person. Jesus was someone who said to me, "Richard, because I live, you shall live also" (John 14:19). Jesus was someone who's the same "yesterday, today, and forever" (Hebrews 13:8). My life changed when Jesus became real to *me!*

Now I don't believe there's anything wrong with being a nightclub singer in Las Vegas, don't get

me wrong. It's just that that wasn't what God had
for my life. And deep down on the inside of me I
knew it wasn't.

God had replaced that dream by putting a new
dream in my heart to serve *Him* through my singing...and I could hardly wait to tell Dad what
had happened!

Dad was just getting ready to launch back into
television after having been off the air for almost
two years. The old program format had been in
black and white. But this time he was going to
produce the programs in color and he would make
the programs in Los Angeles and ship them to
several hundred stations across the country. I knew
he'd want me to be an integral part of all this and
I was finally ready.

That afternoon after praying with Mother, I
picked up the telephone and called Dad. I told him
what had just happened to me and how I felt. And
I said, "Dad, everything's going to be fine. You'll
see when you get home."

When Dad finished the crusade in California
and flew back to Tulsa, he and I sat down together
for the first time in a long time and prayed together
and worked out our differences man to man. We
each asked forgiveness of the other for things we'd
done to hurt each other. Dad and I got our relationship back on track that day. I knew that God
was calling me to join the Oral Roberts Ministry
team — not because I was Oral Roberts' son, but
because God was calling *me,* Richard Roberts, to
serve Him in that way. I'll never forget turning to
Dad to say, "Dad, I used to think you were on my

back. But now we're standing side by side."

It was a miracle as great as any he or I have ever known.

Yet I knew it was only the beginning of a life-long relationship with the GOD OF A SECOND CHANCE.

What About You?

Would you like to meet this GOD OF A SECOND CHANCE for yourself? Would you like to have the power in your life to change those things that you know aren't right? The Bible says that when we seek God with our whole heart we *will* find Him. (See Deuteronomy 4:29.) It also says that when you accept Jesus Christ as your personal Lord and Savior, "old things pass away; behold, ALL things become new" (2 Corinthians 5:17). *You* can have a brand-new life today when you accept Jesus into your heart. You can have a SECOND CHANCE to make your life what you've always wanted it to be. Let me lead you in a simple prayer of confession. Will you say this prayer out loud:

"Oh, Lord, be merciful to me a sinner. I'm a sinner, Lord, and I know it. I ask Your forgiveness for all the wrong things I've done in my life and I ask You to cleanse me of my sin. Lord, I believe that You sent Your Son Jesus to die on the cross for me and I accept Him now as my *personal* Lord and Savior. Jesus, I invite You to come into my life today and to make my life what You would have it to be. Thank You, Lord, for dying for me, for loving me, and for giving me a *second chance*. And in Jesus' name, I *am* going to make it! Amen and amen."

Oh, I know you're praying that prayer and accepting Jesus Christ into your heart as your personal Lord and Savior. I believe that the greatest miracle of all is the salvation of a soul . . . because only God knows what He can do with a life that is truly "sold out" to Him.

I want to give you a little booklet I've prepared that will help you know what to do next in your new walk with the Lord. In the back of this book is a page you can fill out and send back to me requesting my booklet. I love you and want to know what has happened to you through reading this book so that I can rejoice with you. Let me be the first to say to you: "Welcome to the family of God!"

IV.

Not Perfect...
Just Forgiven

At the beginning of this book, I told you that I want to be completely honest with you about my life...that I'm a human being just like any other human being...and that as a human being I've made many mistakes. It certainly would not be honest to let you think that just because I accepted Christ that I somehow became immune from making any more mistakes. Just a few weeks after accepting Christ, I made what became possibly the biggest and most serious mistake of my life.

But, thank God, that's not the end of the story. Because through that experience of many years of suffering and heartache, I came to know the love and grace of God in a way I might never have known otherwise.

When I accepted Jesus in 1968 at the age of 19, I was as naive as most people are about what it really means to be a Christian and to "walk out" your Christian life. I thought that everything just automatically became perfect, no matter what I did or what decisions I made.

I soon found out differently. Just about one

month after accepting Christ, I got married.

I know now that at that point in my life I really didn't understand love. I didn't understand what a relationship was all about. All I knew was that I wanted to be married and I went after it. Never mind that I went against my parents' wishes and against the advice and prayers of my friends. I wanted to get married and I got married.

I was young and I thought I had all the answers to life. Of course, I didn't have.

I soon realized that I had made a terrible mistake. But I didn't know how to get out of it. I didn't believe in divorce. *So I decided to make my marriage work.* And for the next ten years I really worked at making it work. I did everything I knew to do.

I was very heavily involved at that time in my dad's television work. We had just begun the new format of Sunday morning *Oral Roberts and You* half-hour programs. We were producing national prime-time "Contact" specials every quarter. This was long before we had any TV studio or equipment of our own at Oral Roberts University. We taped our weekly programs in Los Angeles and often traveled to different locations around the world for our prime-time quarterly specials. We taped in Japan, England, Canada, Alaska, and Hawaii, just to name a few of the places. After we bought our own TV equipment we began taping many of our specials right on the Oral Roberts University campus.

I was also instrumental in the formation and direction of our television singers — a group of ORU students called the World Action Singers. The World

Action Singers had actually evolved out of another student group known as the ORU Collegians, which was the first music ministry team to come out of ORU. The ORU Collegians had traveled overseas with my dad to many foreign countries where he was conducting crusades.

The newly formed World Action Singers became my responsibility. I was the director of the group as well as the featured soloist.

At that time I wasn't aware of any calling into a preaching ministry or a healing ministry. I was a singer and so I sang. But in addition to singing on the TV programs, I also produced and made some 15 record albums — both solo albums and albums of the World Action Singers — usually from music that had come out of our television programs. When I was not involved in TV work, I traveled and gave concerts literally around the world wherever I was invited.

Meanwhile, during all the busyness of our lives, I was trying to make my marriage work. After a few years Christi, our first daughter, came along... then Juli, our second daughter, came about a year later.

But things just continued to deteriorate in our marriage. I knew I was serving the Lord to the best of my ability in my dad's ministry. I also knew I was hurting and torn up on the inside as I tried to sing and minister to the needs of other people. I felt torn apart but I just didn't know what else to do.

Finally, in 1978 after ten years, the marriage ended... and I went through one of the hardest

experiences of my life. Divorce is an experience
that more than 50 percent of the families in this
nation have been through or are going through
right now as I write this to you. I know what it
means to go through a divorce. And though I had
not been the one to file the divorce papers or seek
the divorce, I knew I had to accept my part of the
blame. I knew that to be fair I had to admit that
there were mistakes made on both sides of the
relationship and I had to admit my own part in
the failure of our marriage.

Of course, I can't adequately describe the agony
a person suffers through divorce. I felt like I'd
been to hell and back. *I had failed just about as
miserably as a man can fail... and I knew it.* I had
married the wrong person and I suffered from that
decision for more than ten years. I knew that other
people had suffered from it too. In that respect
my divorce was no different from anyone else's.
But something happened to me in my divorce that
doesn't happen to most people... something that
could have made that time in my life unbearable
if it had not been for a family who believed in me in
spite of my mistakes and in a SECOND-CHANCE
GOD who never once gave up on me.

When *my* divorce happened, it hit 300 newspapers nationwide... and everyone knew that
Richard Roberts had failed.

When that happened, I wanted to crawl in a hole
somewhere and pull the hole in after me. I wanted
to get on an airplane and fly to the farthest corner
of the world and change my name. I wanted to
die... I prayed to die.

But, you know, I didn't die... I lived! And what
are you going to do then? When you die, it's very
simple because you just go to heaven to be with
Jesus. But when you live it's a different story.
Then you have to deal with the failure and find a
way of going on with your life.

So I got down on my knees before the Lord,
and I admitted my failure. I accepted my part of
the blame and told God that I was sorry for what
I'd done. I'd missed His ideal for my life and I
knew it. But I also knew the Bible says that when
we confess our sins to God, "he is faithful and just
to forgive us our sins, and to cleanse us from all
unrighteousness" (1 John 1:9).

I discovered the good thing about making a
mistake is that you can say, "God, I'm sorry for
what I've done. Help me not to do it again." And
if you are truly sorry and truly repent — which
simply means to make the decision in your mind to
turn around or to *turn away from your sin* — God
will give you a SECOND CHANCE with your
life. I know He will because that's what He did
for me the moment I asked Him to.

The very first thing God did after I'd asked
His forgiveness was to say to me, *Richard, get up
off your knees and stand up straight.*

And that shocked me. Because I knew that
many people who knew about my divorce wanted
to throw me out with the garbage. Some of them
had written to me and some had written to my dad
telling him to disown me... that I had no right
to be involved in the leadership of a ministry now
that I was divorced. Yet, here was God telling me

to quit feeling ashamed and to go on with my life.

Through that experience I learned one of the most valuable lessons I could ever have learned. *I learned that even though people judge you, God forgives you.* That's the kind of God He is. And finally it began to sink in that maybe my life wasn't over after all! Maybe God had something more He wanted me to do.

When it dawned on me that God wasn't through with Richard Roberts — in spite of what *people* might say — I picked myself up off the floor and decided to go on with my life.

Now did you hear that, friend? I said that *I* did the picking up. God had forgiven me and given me a SECOND CHANCE, but it was Richard Roberts who had to make the decision to pick himself up and go on.

Sure, it was hard. It was probably the hardest thing I've ever had to do. There were times when the criticism about me was very heavy. There were times when I felt like giving up. And maybe I would have given up had it not been for my own determination to start my life over and for a loving, supportive family who believed in me.

I had learned as a little boy from watching my dad deal with criticism against his ministry that when people strike at you, you don't strike back at them. Because when you strike back, it only brings you down to their level and it is not uplifting to the name of Jesus. Sure, I *felt* like striking back sometimes. I knew there were things I could tell that would make people understand my side of the divorce. In any situation there are always circumstances beyond your control that other people aren't aware of. And sometimes it takes every ounce of control you have to keep quiet.

But the Lord had spoken to me very clearly to keep my mouth shut and not to share the personal details of that relationship or the divorce. And I simply didn't... and *don't*... intend to share them.

Instead, I learned to love the people who were criticizing me and to pray for them. I realized that many of them were condemning me because of the judgmental teaching they'd had. They weren't bad people; they just didn't know any better. Maybe they didn't know the God I know... the GOD OF A SECOND CHANCE... the God who is a good God... the God who cares about the individual... the God who deals with human beings and counts them more important than any institution.

And who can resist a God like that? Certainly *I* couldn't.

Even though I'd been a Christian for more than ten years, during the next 12 months I began to study my Bible like I never had before. And I came to know the Lord in a way I'd never known. In Philippians 3:10 St. Paul said, "That I may know him [Christ], and the power of his resurrection, *and the fellowship of his suffering...*"

And through a time of intense personal suffering, I *knew* Him. I took heart from the message of a SECOND CHANCE that runs so clearly throughout the New Testament.

To my amazement, there seemed to be Scriptures that I'd never really seen before, maybe because I'd never really needed them before. I

especially remember reading the story in John 4
about the woman at the well whom Jesus encountered as He passed through Samaria. She knew
from the moment He asked her to draw Him a
drink of water from the well that Jesus was different from the other Jews she had known, because
normally Jews had no dealings with Samaritans.
After Jesus had drunk the water, He told her something very strange . . . that it should have been she
who was asking Him for a drink of the water of life
that only He could give.

And somehow, miraculously, this woman at the
well knew that she needed what Jesus had to offer.
When she said, "Lord, give me this water, that I
may thirst not, neither come hither to draw," Jesus
said to her, "Go, call thy husband, and come hither."

Well, the woman had no husband and she told
Jesus so. And Jesus answered her saying, "Thou
hast well said, I have no husband: For thou hast
had five husbands; and he whom thou now hast is
not thy husband: in that saidst thou truly." (See
John 4:15-18.) Yet I noticed that Jesus chose to
reveal himself to this woman and to forgive her of
her sins. And when her life was changed, Jesus
didn't condemn her. He sent her into town to
tell others about Him . . . to be an evangelist of
the gospel!

And the more I studied the Bible and came to
know the SECOND-CHANCE nature of God, the
more I purposed in my heart to follow *His* will for
my life for the rest of my life.

What About You?

Are you wrestling with a situation where people are condemning you for what you've done, even though you know in your heart that you did the very best you knew to do at the time? Are you "lying down" on the inside... "parking" beside your failure? If you are, remember that even though people judge you, *God* forgives you. Somewhere along the line, you have to make up your mind about whether you're going to listen to what people think or to what God thinks. It's up to *you* to reach out and take the forgiveness He offers and start seeing yourself as God sees you: *forgiven.*

That's why I said that after my divorce, Richard Roberts had to pick *himself* up; God didn't do it for me. I had to make a *decision of my will* about my life. I had to answer the question: Was I going to "park" beside my failure for the rest of my life because of what people said about me, or was I going to climb up out of the pit I was in and let God make something out of my life? The decision was mine. I knew that *God* would... if *I* would.

Sure, it was hard. It's still hard. I don't enjoy talking about the mistakes I've made. But, friend, if it can help you with *your* life or if it can bring even one person to know the Lord, it's *worth* it!

Don't ever forget that in your problems and your struggles, there are always other people watching you. They're waiting to see what you're going to do with your life. Are you going to give up or are you going to go on with the Lord? If your faith in

Jesus is real, it will work in the hard times as well as in the good times of life. Your getting up and going on with the Lord, in spite of your faults and failures, will show people that God is real.

Let me share something with you that happened because I ignored what people said against me and went on with what I knew God was calling me to do.

After my divorce and remarriage, there was a man in this country who was vehemently against me. He actually spent time preaching against me all across America. People sometimes sent me transcripts of what he said about me . . . even to using my name as part of his public sermons.

But, you know, I never hated that man. I just prayed for him and went on with my life.

Then one day about two years ago, this man showed up in Tulsa on the Oral Roberts University campus and asked if he could see me. When I agreed, he came to my office and got down on his knees in front of me. He said that he'd heard me tell the story of the hundreds and thousands of people that I'd won to Christ in my crusades in Africa and of the outstanding miracles of healing that had happened there.

He mentioned specifically one 22-year-old Nigerian boy, Abdul, whose story he had heard. Abdul had been crippled from birth. Everyone in Abdul's town of Jos knew him because he sat in front of the post office building every day and begged for his living.

Then one night Abdul came to my crusade in Jos and was gloriously healed by the power of God as I prayed.

Well, the crusade crowd of about 20,000 people almost exploded! Abdul's healing touched the entire city of Jos for the Lord. Their friend, whom they had watched crawl on his hands and knees all of his life, now stood in front of their very eyes, walking! It was just like many of the miracles in the Bible.

That miraculous report of healing had dramatically touched this man who had been preaching against me. With tears streaming down his cheeks, he told me that the Lord had rebuked him and told him that he was wrong.

Then he said something wonderful to me. He said, "Richard, I have seen the fruit of your ministry and I now know I've been wrong about you. Please forgive me."

We embraced... and I told him how much I appreciated his coming, but that I had never held it against him because I knew that was not what Jesus would have done.

To this day, that man and I are tremendous friends in the Lord.

That's why I say that until you try it, you'll never know what a great impact your decision to go on with the Lord and with your life may have on someone else. I believe God will begin to use you to minister to the needs of other people in a way you've never known before!

V.

A Second Chance at Love

When I found myself single again after my divorce, I made up my mind that I was not going to make another mistake. I decided I would keep myself clean before the Lord and walk uprightly before Him. I was very cautious about where I went and whom I was with. I knew there would be all kinds of untrue rumors circulating about me no matter what I did, but I determined never to get in a bad situation where someone could honestly accuse me of something wrong.

It wasn't easy, believe me. At the age of 30 I was still a young man with the normal desires that any young man has. After a while I began to pray that the Lord would send a woman into my life so that I might someday have a marriage of love, honor, and respect on both sides. I prayed God would send me someone I could support and who would support me and the work that God had called me to do. By this time the Lord was also dealing with me about a preaching ministry in addition to my singing. And during the time that I was single I did answer God's call to preach with a resounding

YES. A great anointing came upon me to preach
and teach God's Word. I knew I wanted a wife
who would fully support me in the *full* call that
God had on my life.

While all this was going on in *my* life, God began
dealing with a young woman far away in Florida.
Her name? Lindsay Salem.

Lindsay's family had lived in Michigan when
she was a little girl. They had been Partners with
the Oral Roberts Ministry for years. Her father
became ill with cancer and died when she was 12.
Mr. Salem had been friends with my dad's close
associate in the ministry, Lee Braxton, and before
Mr. Salem died, Lee had arranged for my dad to
phone Mr. Salem and to pray for him while he was
in the hospital.

Lindsay's family was very close-knit and, of
course, her father's death was very difficult for her
to handle. During that time in her life, she began
watching my dad regularly on TV. She began writing
letters to him and became a Partner with him in
his ministry. In fact, she has always said that if it
had not been for my dad's teaching, she might not
have made it through that difficult time as a teenager without her father. Of course, I didn't know
any of these things until we met many years later.

After her father's death, her family moved to
Florida. Lindsay went to high school and college
there. She graduated from Rollins College in 1978
with very good grades and a desire to go on to law
school. From the time she was just a little girl,
Lindsay had dreamed of becoming a lawyer. But
she wanted to go to a law school where the teaching

wouldn't conflict with her faith in Jesus Christ. She knew that until Oral Roberts University's O. W. Coburn School of Law opened in 1979 — one year later — there was no other law school she would feel comfortable attending.

So Lindsay worked in a law office for a year and got as much practical experience as she could while she waited for the ORU law school to open. She applied and was accepted. In August 1979, she got in her car and drove from Winter Park, Florida, to Tulsa, Oklahoma, to be part of the first class in the O. W. Coburn School of Law.

On the way to Tulsa, the Lord began speaking to her about a young man named Richard Roberts.

Now you've got to remember that Lindsay had *always* wanted to go to law school and become a lawyer. She had absolutely no desire to get married at that point in her life. She was completely taken by surprise when the Lord kept bringing my name and my face before her during her *long* drive to Tulsa. (One of Lindsay's talents doesn't happen to be in reading maps and her trip ended up being a lot longer than it should have been!)

Well, of course, she couldn't figure out why thoughts about me kept coming to her. As a teenager watching my dad's program on TV, she had viewed me as an older, married man. (Actually, I'm only seven years older than Lindsay.) She had seen me on TV just a few times since she had learned that I was divorced. Each time she seemed to sense a deep loneliness about me... that I'd been through something very painful. All she could decide was that perhaps the Lord wanted her to help me get over whatever I'd been through that was so painful.

And to show you how the Lord is capable of bringing those people into our lives that He intends to be there, Lindsay had not been on campus more than a few days before she met a law-school class-mate who just "happened" to be a good friend of mine.

By this time, Lindsay was beginning to feel a very strong attraction to me. The Lord had con-tinued to bring my face and my name to her mind every day. So one night during the first week of school, my friend arranged for Lindsay and me to meet after a service in which I preached to the ORU students, faculty, and staff.

I preached on the story of David and Goliath. During my sermon, I asked those in the audience to think of the three biggest giants, or problems, that they were facing in their lives. Then I prayed for those three needs to be met.

After the service, I went backstage to meet this girl from Florida that my friend had been telling me about. He introduced us and immediately I noticed how attractive she was. She said that she had really enjoyed my message and I said to her, "What did you enjoy about it?"

"I liked the part about your biggest giant," she replied.

So I said back to her, "What's *your* biggest giant?" It seemed like a mild enough question to ask someone who had just started law school. But when I heard her answer, I was never so shocked in my life. She looked straight into my eyes and said, "YOU are."

I think I literally took a step backward when it sunk in what she'd said. As I smiled and tried to be polite, I looked over at my friend as if to say, "Thanks a lot for introducing me to this nut!"

We stood there for another couple of minutes and then I excused myself and walked away with my friend. As we walked out the door I said, "Why did you introduce me to *her*? What have I ever done to her? I've never even seen her before tonight!" We both just kind of laughed and went on . . . and I thought that was the end of that!

But as the days began to pass, I found that I couldn't stand the suspense any longer. I *had* to know just what that girl meant by saying that I was her biggest giant. Lindsay was living over in our graduate housing community with all the other graduate students, so I just picked up the phone, got her phone number, and called her to find out what I'd done to cause that response.

And wouldn't you know it . . . she wasn't there!

I did talk with her roommate and found out that Lindsay was out playing tennis and would be back later. So a few hours later, I called again and this time I got her.

After I told her who was calling, I said, "Will you please explain to me your remark the other night about my being your biggest giant?"

And rather reluctantly she began to tell me the story of how for some time the Lord had been bringing my name and my face to her mind. She told me how she had been praying for me and how she had only recently learned that I was divorced.

She told me that in the last few months as she watched me on TV she had seen the loneliness in my face and that the Lord must have placed a special burden on her heart for me.

Well, I still didn't really know what she was talking about. So I said, "Well, then what do you mean that I'm your biggest problem?"

And she said, "Richard, you don't understand at all. I've dreamed of being a lawyer all my life. I want to go to law school and then practice law . . . that's why I came here. But the Lord keeps dealing with me that I'm to have some kind of relationship with you. And if that happens, it's going to throw all of my plans clear off."

And thinking of how unusual our relationship had already been, I said to her, "Well, I'm not so sure I *want* a relationship with you."

But we both decided that we'd like to meet again, so I asked her out. Lindsay and I had our first date on August 27, 1979.

Lindsay and I have been married for more than five years now, and she still tells me and other people that she fell in love with me the very first night we went out. Now that was hard for her to reconcile. She even asked the Lord, "How could You let me fall in love with Richard Roberts when You know I've had a dream all my life of being a lawyer?" She knew enough about my life and my work for the Lord to know that if she married me someday, the law career she had always dreamed of would just not be compatible with being my wife.

But more than anything else, Lindsay loved the Lord and wanted *His* will for her life. She knew that whatever plan He had for her life would be where she would find the most fulfillment. She never would have married me without knowing that it was God's will for her.

On the other hand, I was facing the same hesitation that Lindsay was, but for very different reasons. Having been through a divorce the year before, I was really seeking the Lord about this new relationship. I knew that if I were to remarry, all hell would probably break loose from all sides. Some critics would probably come out of the woodwork who, until then, had not spoken up about my divorce. I also knew that in any future marriage, I needed to have a *Bible wife* in every sense of the word. I needed a wife who would stand beside me in the ministry and who would understand and support God's calling on my life. I also had to know that our relationship was what *God* had for my life, not just what Richard Roberts thought he wanted.

Lindsay and I shared these feelings with each other and prayed about it many times during the months we dated. We were absolutely certain that any future happiness we might have together would depend upon our *first* knowing that *God* had brought us together and that He intended for us to be man and wife.

I want to share with you how God confirmed over and over to us that our relationship had been ordained of Him.

The first thing that happened involved Lindsay's family. When I took her back to her apartment after our first date she called her mother. She's very close to her family, as I am to mine, and she wanted to tell them what had happened.

Up until this time she had not told her mom anything about meeting me. But when her mother answered the phone and Lindsay said, "Mom, guess where I went tonight?" her mother very calmly replied, "You went out with Richard Roberts."

Well, needless to say, Lindsay was shocked.

"How in the world did you know that?" she asked.

"Well, I pray to the same Lord you do, Lindsay. And He told me that that's what you'd be doing tonight."

What a surprise! But I think it really helped Lindsay to know that God had already spoken to her mother about us. She has a great deal of confidence in her mom's judgment and I think their conversation about our date eased her mind that this was indeed of God.

Lindsay and I began dating regularly and our relationship seemed to flourish from the beginning. During my divorce and the months after, I had suffered from an ulcer. I had been on medication for it and yet it would continually flare up. I prayed about it and others prayed for me, but I couldn't seem to get completely healed. Sometimes the medicine would work and sometimes it wouldn't. But within the first two weeks of our dating, my ulcer completely disappeared.

After about three months of dating, I knew that I was beginning to fall in love with Lindsay. That concerned me. Not because of any questions I had about her feelings for *me,* because Lindsay was a

different type of woman than I had ever met before.
She genuinely cared about me. Not because I was
Oral Roberts' son, but because I was *me.*

All through my life I had encountered people
who wanted something from me or thought I could
do something for them just because I was Oral
Roberts' son. And I was always concerned about
the people who wanted to be close to me for that
reason. You could say that I had become somewhat
skeptical of people because of what I'd been through
with certain people trying to use me in relationships. Lindsay understood that. By her loving me
just for myself, she helped me break down those
walls of skepticism.

No, it wasn't her feelings for me that had me
concerned. But I was worried about the hard road
of criticism that was facing us if we married. I
began to pray about it.

By this time I was 31 years old and I wanted
to be married again and have a family. In my heart
of hearts I knew that God is not a God of punishment, but of mercy. And that just because I'd made
a mistake when I was very young, He would not
punish me for the rest of my life. I didn't believe
that He wanted me to live as a single man always
subject to temptation . . . always battling that I
wouldn't make a mistake as I traveled around the
world ministering and having the opportunity to
meet many attractive women.

So I began to ask God what He wanted me to
do about my life. This was very serious to me and
I needed an answer.

"God, do You *want* me to live alone for the rest

With me are (left to right) my dad, my older brother Ronnie (who died in 1982), my little sister Roberta, my mother, my grandmother Mamma Roberts, and my older sister Rebecca (who died in 1977).

Photo courtesy of Industrial Photo Service

Our family lived on a farm for several years when I was a boy and one of my dad's favorite pastimes was riding horses. I loved the times when Dad would take me along and let me ride with him on his horse.

I started singing at a very early age and sometimes sang publicly in my dad's crusades. But when I was a teenager, I decided not to sing for my dad or for the Lord anymore. I was going to use my talent to be a nightclub singer in Las Vegas.

Dad was on the road most of the time when I was your but when he was home he always made time to read God's Word to us each day. He made the Bible come alive to Roberta and me.

I'll never forget the day ORU was dedicated. My brother
(who was in the service) and sisters and I knew it was the
fulfillment of a dream for my dad. I was happy for him,
but until God changed my heart several years later, ORU
was the last place in the world I wanted to go to college!

Here I am with
actress Shirley Jones
at the Starlight
Theater in Kansas
City. I was on my way
to a singing career
and no one was going
to change my mind.

Here I am with Dad standing outside one of the buildings on the ORU campus that overlooks the Prayer Tower. This photo was taken just shortly after I returned to ORU as a student.

After I started working with Dad in the ministry, I sometimes helped him pray for the sick in his services. But it wasn't until 1980 that I really began to see results when I prayed for people. That's when the anointing of God came upon me to begin speaking out the word of faith for people's healing.

During the seventies I was very involved with my dad's TV work both as a featured soloist and in the formation and direction of our World Action Singers. Tennessee Ernie Ford was a guest on several of our programs.

For our prime-time "Contact" specials, we often traveled to beautiful locations around the world, including this special filmed in Japan.

Many people still remember the "Contact" special we filmed in Alaska. It was one of the last ones we did on location.

Photo courtesy of Lee Salem, Krofft Productions

It was a wonderful day when Dad laid his hands on me to ordain me as a minister of the gospel of Jesus Christ. What a work God had done in my heart since the time I told Dad to get off my back and out of my life. I'm proud to say that today Oral and Richard Roberts are a father-and-son healing team for Jesus Christ.

In January 1980, Lindsay and I were married. I can't tell you how grateful I am to have a wife who is beside me and who supports me in my calling from God.

Sometimes I will still go out into the crowds at my crusades to lay hands on someone who is sick and needs to be healed. Often when someone has been in a wheelchair for some time, I try to take a little extra time in my ministry to them to encourage them to believe for their miracle.

During the healing services I often have people who are healed give a word of testimony. If they were on crutches and couldn't walk without them — as this lady was — I may ask them to hold the crutches up to encourage the faith of other people who are still believing for their healing.

Shortly after the death of our son Richard Oral in January of 1984, Lindsay and I conducted a month-long crusade in Africa. God honored our commitment and we saw more miracles than we'd ever seen before. The crowds were so tightly packed together that when someone on crutches was healed, their crutches were sometimes passed through the crowd up to the platform. The crutches would arrive long before the person who had been using them!

You can see from this photo just how large and tightly packed the crowds were during our African crusade. The African robe I am wearing was given to me as an honor to wear as I preached and to bring home with me to America.

We had tremendous response overseas every time I gave those attending the crusades an opportunity to accept Jesus into their hearts. Through the years in my crusades, it's not been unusual to see two thirds of the crowd raise their hand or stand to accept the Lord.

When God gives me a message to preach and the anointing of the Holy Spirit is on me, like here in Jamaica, I become almost like a different person and I speak with an authority that comes from God alone. It's that **anointing** that breaks the yoke of bondage in people's lives and brings them God's deliverance.

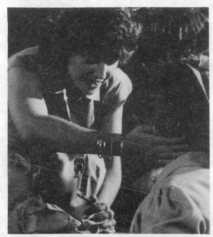

For several years, God has been using Lindsay more and more to pray for people's healings. Often while I am praying for people from the platform in my crusades, Lindsay will go out among the crowd to lay her hands on people and pray. In one of my overseas crusades, she walked knee-deep in mud in order to pray for the people standing in the rain-soaked field.

During one of my crusades in Canada, this little boy from Pakistan experienced a healing in his left ear. His hearing had been injured from measles earlier in his life. When he realized that Jesus had healed him he came forward to sit with me and tell the people what God had done.

*Lindsay is with me almost every day on the **RICHARD ROBERTS** show and she plays a vital role in helping me minister to people's needs. Many people have written in to tell me how much they love and appreciate her on the program and how, oftentimes, God has used a word of Lindsay's to bring about a healing in their life.*

In September 1984, we went on the air live with the **RICHARD ROBERTS** show. This program has given us the opportunity to go with the message of the gospel into thousands more homes than ever before.

I'm always happy to have my dad and mother come on my program as guests because I know that they will always have a good word from the Lord to bring to people who are watching.

I have been honored to have many, many wonderful guests come on my program, such as my dear friend Evangelist Mike Murdock in this photo. My guests are men and women who know Jesus and want to help me spread the message of His SECOND CHANCE.

Since my program began in 1984, we have had to expand our number of prayer partners in the Abundant Life Prayer Group to 60. Here is just a small group of them who help me pray for people on the set every day who call in with desperate needs.

One of the most important times in our program every day is the time Lindsay and I spend with our guests praying over the prayer requests that have come that day. We lay our hands on the large stacks of prayer requests knowing that each sheet represents a human being watching at home who needs a miracle in their life.

When the cameras go off every day on the RICHARD ROBERTS show, the miracles still go on! My team and I, and often our special guest for that day, take special time after each program to minister to the needs of those in our live studio audience. We've seen many people saved and healed during that time.

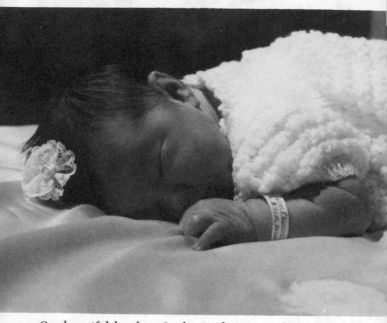

Our beautiful daughter, Jordan Lindsay, is caught napping just a few days after her birth! She's a miracle of God and the joy of our life.

of my life and live a life of celibacy?" I asked Him. Because I was willing to do that if I really knew that was what He wanted me to do.

But I also said, "God, I don't believe You want me to be lonely and miserable. I believe that You are THE GOD OF A SECOND CHANCE. You were the God of a Second Chance when Peter denied You three times while Your life was on trial. And I believe that if Judas had only run to the cross and thrown his arms around Your feet and cried, 'Jesus, I'm sorry for selling You out. I know I made a mistake; please forgive me,' that You would have been the God of a Second Chance for Judas as well."

And I thought again about the Samaritan woman at the well who had had five husbands ... but after she came to the Lord Jesus, He sent her into the town to be an evangelist. He didn't condemn her to a life of hiding from her past.

And suddenly the most wonderful feeling came over me that even if people were against me, God was *for* me! God didn't want me to be unhappy or alone for the rest of my life. He knew that the anointing to preach was growing upon me and that I needed a wife who would be a helpmate to me.

It was a wonderful realization. And Lindsay and I began talking about marriage. I asked her if she thought she was prepared for the onslaught of criticism — the backlash that she would receive as my wife — from people who might misunderstand my remarriage, maybe even from people who were close to us.

Lindsay said that she knew she would have the

support of her family and that would make a
tremendous difference to her in coping with the
criticism. I knew that I would have the love and
support of *my* family as well. Over and over again
they had proven their belief in me in the past,
and I knew they would support my decision to
marry Lindsay.

You see, I'd handled things the right way this
time. I had purposefully planned times when
Lindsay could be around my parents so they could
spend time with her and really get to know her.
And I knew that they felt good about our relationship. Lindsay had made sure that I got to know
her mother also, and I knew she felt good about
our relationship as well. We *knew* we would have
their support and I can't tell you what a difference
that made knowing what we would have to face.

As we were planning and talking about the
future, something really incredible happened to us
that was impossible for us to ignore.

Lindsay and I always attended the twice-weekly
chapel services at ORU during the time we were
dating — but not together. She would sit with the
other graduate students and I would sit up on the
platform with those in the administration of the
university. Now you have to remember that at
this point only a very few people knew we were
even dating, much less how serious our relationship had become. We were still very much in the
process of talking and praying about the possibility
of marriage.

Our chapel speaker one day in the fall of 1979
was Evangelist Kenneth Hagin. He certainly was

not one of the people who knew!

After he preached in our chapel service and while the entire faculty, student body, and administration were still present, the Spirit of prophecy — one of the nine gifts of the Spirit mentioned in 1 Corinthians 12 — came upon him. Now I had known Brother Hagin for many years. He was a man I deeply loved and admired and in whose ministry I believed. I'd seen him prophesy many times in my life and I knew that when he was operating in the office of the prophet, as he was at that moment, I'd never seen him wrong. The prophecy was always "right on."

But this time as he prophesied, he turned to *me*. And though he didn't speak in specifics, I knew exactly what he was talking about. He said to me, "That thing which you have been praying about doing, and you've been concerned about what people are going to think and say and do, *it is of God*. Do it and don't worry about what they think or say or do."

Well, I looked out in the crowd where Lindsay was sitting and she looked like she was going to slide underneath her seat! We were probably the only two people in the building who knew what Brother Hagin was talking about, and she knew *exactly* what he meant . . . and she knew that I knew.

Without a shadow of a doubt, we both knew that it was right in the sight of the Lord for us to be married. That day in chapel, I didn't feel led to go up to Brother Hagin and talk to him about the prophetic message he had given to me. Lindsay and I both just accepted it as being a confirmation

from the Lord. But after we were married I had
the chance to talk to him about it one day. I said,
"Brother Hagin, I know there are many times when
the Spirit of prophecy comes upon you or other
men and women of God and you bring a word from
the Lord to someone's life, and later you are often
not aware of all that you said. That day in chapel
when you gave the word of prophecy to me, did
you know the ramifications of what the Lord was
having you say?"

A big grin came across his face and he said,
"Well, Richard, I'll tell you this. I could have even
told you her name. But I didn't think it was appro-
priate right then."

What a wonderful confirmation from the Lord
Brother Hagin's word of prophecy had been to us.
We both knew that he didn't know Lindsay; he'd
never even met her. But God used him to tell us that
the marriage plans we had made were good plans.

So with the peace of God in our hearts we set
the date for our wedding...January 11, 1980.
Lindsay finished the fall semester in law school
and flew home to Florida to be with her family and
complete the details of our wedding. We were still
keeping our plans very quiet and she had not said
anything to anyone on campus about dropping out
of law school. But she knew that the deepest desire
of her heart was to be my wife and to help me in
the ministry that was continuing to grow in me.

From Florida, she called the director of Admissions at ORU and said, "I'm officially withdrawing
from ORU. Law school is just not for me." But she
didn't tell them the other reason...the fact that

she and I would be getting married in just a few weeks.

So Lindsay was committed to our marriage. And for the next two or three weeks she waited for me to come to Florida for our wedding, not knowing for sure whether Richard Roberts would show up!

Lindsay knew that I was deeply concerned about the criticism we would encounter after we married. She knew there might still be the possibility that I would back out of our plans at the last minute. She says now that she was never so relieved in her life as the night when the plane landed in Orlando and, as people started getting off the plane, she saw a pair of cowboy boots coming down the stairs . . . and she knew they were *my* cowboy boots!

What she *didn't* know that night was that there had been a chance that I might not have come, even up to the last few days. After she had gone home to Florida, I had spent time with the leadership of the Oral Roberts Ministry talking to them about my desire to remarry. It was one of the hardest things I've ever done but I wanted them to know that I cared about how they felt about our plans. I went to them individually and privately and asked them to pray with me that the Lord would lead me in my final decision.

Then I gathered the leaders of the university, the City of Faith, and the evangelistic association, of which I am the president, together in a private meeting several days before I was to fly to Florida to meet Lindsay. I asked them to keep everything we were talking and praying about confidential. I said to them, "I realize that you don't really have the right to say 'no' about my remarriage. But as my colaborers in the ministry, I'm giving you that right. I'm asking for your blessing on our marriage ...but I will abide by your decision."

And I meant it. I felt this was one last confirmation that Lindsay and I really needed to have before we married.

To my joy, they came and threw their arms around me and really applauded me for keeping my life right before the Lord in that year that I'd been single. In essence, they said, "We've seen you and Lindsay together and we have a good feeling about this marriage. We support you 100 percent. Of course, you have our blessing."

Finally, in my eyes, there were no more hurdles to our being married as soon as possible. My family felt good about it, Lindsay's family felt good about it, and the top people in our ministry felt good about it. So, without announcing it to anyone, I got on an airplane and flew to Florida and we were married in the chapel of the Rollins College campus on January 11, 1980.

God had not only given me a SECOND CHANCE at living, He had given me a SECOND CHANCE at love.

What About You?

In whatever failure you're facing, have you accepted your part of the blame yet? Have you admitted to yourself and to God that you made a mistake? Maybe you have a long history of making bad decisions in your life and you think that God can never forgive you and give you a SECOND CHANCE. Friend, I believe with all my heart and I speak with the confidence of knowing what the Word of God says, that there is *nothing* you could have done or ever will do that God cannot...and *will* not forgive. *If* you ask Him to.

You see, God can never forgive you if you don't get down on your knees and ask Him to. That's something that He cannot do for you. God has already done His part in making forgiveness available to you when He sent Jesus to the cross. Now you have to do your part and reach out and receive that forgiveness. You may want to pour out your heart to Him about the years of mistakes in your life. Or it may be as simple as just saying one or two words that you mean from the bottom of your heart...such as, "Jesus...O.K.!"

That's what a guest on my daily TV program said to the Lord when he knew he could no longer make it in his life without Him. He had fought and rebelled against God for many years as a young man and his life was in a mess.

But one day after years and years of pain, that young man came to the end of himself...just as you may be at the end of yourself right now. And with tears streaming down his cheeks he lifted his hands up to heaven and shouted, "Jesus...O.K.!"

With just two simple words like that, the young man's life was miraculously transformed. He accepted Christ as his Savior and now he's preaching the gospel and praying for the sick and winning thousands of souls to the Lord.

Now that doesn't mean that God is going to call *you* into a healing ministry of your own when you turn your past failures over to Him, but it does mean that He has something more for you to do ... something that's just right for you.

God's not through blessing you, my friend. God's not through giving you the desires of your heart ... or helping you fulfill the dreams you've had all your life.

As I look back now, I see that it was only after my greatest failures that my life really began. And like you, I never would have believed it possible for God to turn things around.

But it happened ... and it's possible for *you,* my friend. It can happen right now ... if you'll take that first step and get down on your knees before God. Ask Him to forgive you and then *believe* that He has.

You can trust God, for He's the God of a SECOND CHANCE.

VI.

The Birth of a Healing Ministry...My Dream Comes True

When Lindsay and I were married, the announcement ran in papers around the country. The Tulsa newspapers picked the story up the next day and just as we knew they would, the critics came out of the woodwork. Now I was not only a person who had been divorced — for which many people felt sympathetic and compassionate — I had done what many people considered the unpardonable sin. I had remarried.

The mail began to pour in from people saying things like, "Richard Roberts, you're going to hell for this and burn forever." Sometimes I jokingly say that when I die, no one will have to preach my funeral service ... because, brother, it's already *been* preached!

But the most important thing for Lindsay and me during this really difficult time after we first married was that we *knew in our hearts* we had done the right thing. *And when you know that, all hell may break loose but you can take it!*

So Lindsay and I took the criticism... with our families' help, knowing that the Bible says, "A soft answer turneth away wrath" (Proverbs 15:1). We didn't hate the people who criticized us and we didn't strike back, because Jesus never struck back. Instead, I took those criticism letters and turned the situation around. I wrote each one of the people a letter explaining my heart to them... and I used their letter as an opportunity to minister God's love to them.

I decided that in spite of *any* criticism that would come... no matter how heavy it might be ... I wasn't going to run away and hide. I would let my light shine for Jesus and pray that I could bring something good out of something that the devil would have liked to use to destroy me. I rededicated my life to God and to the work He had called me to do. "No matter what people do or say or think," I decided, "I'm going to go on with my life and win as many souls to Jesus as I can."

Lindsay's love for me and her commitment to our marriage never wavered an inch during that time. She stood right by my side and was proud to be my wife. I'm sure that in many ways the criticism hurt her worse than it did me, because they were striking at the man she loved. But she never complained.

One reason I wanted to write this book is because I think divorce is a subject that really needs to be dealt with, not just in the secular world but in the body of Christ as well. Statistics show that 50 percent of the marriages in this country are now ending in divorce. And nearly half of the people

in the remaining 50 percent would like to get out
of their marriages. That means that 75 percent of
all marriages in this country are in very bad shape
and many people who have been involved in those
marriages have come out deeply hurt. I believe
that, just like me, they need to be healed of that
hurt. The good news is they can be.

I remember after going through my divorce I
wondered how I could possibly help other people
who were hurting when I needed to be healed
myself. Through my relationship with Lindsay,
God brought much of that healing about. The
wonderful thing too was that after she and I were
married, we began to hear from people who took
heart from my life. Along with the critical letters,
I immediately began receiving letters of encourage-
ment from people who had been divorced and were
now remarried, but who often felt terribly guilty
about what they had done. When they saw how
happy Lindsay and I were, it gave them courage
to believe that God had forgiven them and was
giving them a second chance for a *good* marriage.

I began to minister to hundreds and thousands
of people to let them know that, with Jesus' help,
there *is* life after divorce. It wasn't long before the
Lord began to deal with me about moving into the
healing ministry of praying for people's needs to
be met in every area of their lives.

For several years I had been conducting services
around this country for the Partners of our ministry. I would talk to them about the Lord, and
in recent months, I had begun to preach. But for
most of the service I just sang the songs that God

laid on my heart to sing. And I loved to sing. I still
do. I know there's something very special about a
song that prepares people's hearts to hear the Word
of God. God anointed my singing. People were
often healed while listening to me sing, even though
I never really prayed for the sick *with results*.

Now I knew that God was beginning to open up
a healing ministry to me that I had dreamed of
from the time I had sat in my dad's crusades as a
little boy and watched the people being healed.
For years I had dreamed of it, yet it was a dream
that I was almost afraid to hope for. I just had
trouble believing it could happen to Richard Roberts
and I didn't really know *how* to move into it if it
did happen. My dad had always said he felt the
anointing of God in his right hand, and so he would
lay hands on them as he prayed. I thought maybe
that's what would happen to me someday.

Then about three months after Lindsay and I
were married I was preaching, and as I was closing
the service in prayer, I felt a strong urging to
speak the words, "Lord, heal that man's toe." As
soon as I spoke the words I thought to myself,
*What'd you say that for? And in front of all these
people! Why, that's the silliest thing I've ever heard.*

And not knowing what else to say or do, I just
finished my prayer, closed the service, and flew
back to Tulsa. About a week later I received a
letter from a man who said to me:

"Remember in that service when you said,
'Lord, heal that man's toe'? Well, *I was that
man!* My toe was broken and I'd been to the
doctor to have it x-rayed but there wasn't

much they could do.

"I was sitting there at your crusade. And when you said, 'Lord, heal that man's toe,' *my* toe snapped. Suddenly the pain left and I could move it freely.

"When I got home I went back to the doctor and had it x-rayed again. We put the old X ray up against the new X ray and guess what? My toe was completely healed!"

And then he said to me, "Richard Roberts, what did you do?"

Well, I wrote him back immediately and said, "Sir, I didn't do *anything*. As a matter of fact, I felt stupid when I said that."

That night when I went to bed, I closed my eyes ... and dreamed about a man's big toe! That's the honest truth. Even when I woke up in the middle of the night and sat up in bed, all I could see was a big ol' toe! And for about two weeks, all I dreamed about was a man's big toe.

It was the strangest thing. I just couldn't imagine what was happening to me. The worst part was that I couldn't *tell* anyone what was going on! I wanted to tell Lindsay. But how do you tell your wife that in your dreams all you can see is some man's big toe? I thought she'd probably think I was nuts!

Well, the dream persisted and persisted until finally it began to dawn on me that maybe God was trying to tell me something through my dreams of that man's toe. So I told Lindsay. And when I tell you her reaction, you'll probably understand why I love her so much and why she is such a support to me as my wife.

She *didn't* say, "That's crazy" or "You ought to be dreaming about me."

She said, "Richard, maybe this is the beginning of the healing ministry that you've told me you've dreamed of all your life."

No one had ever said anything like that to me before. No one had encouraged me to believe that my dream could really happen someday. And when she said that, it struck something down on the inside of me.

I said, "Maybe it is."

We joined our hands together right then and I turned to her and said, "Lindsay, all my life, even when I was running away from God, I still felt a closeness to the healing ministry of Jesus Christ. I can remember even as a little boy the tears that would stream down my cheeks when I'd see somebody healed. And as I got older and didn't want God in my life, when I would see a blind eye healed or a deaf ear opened, I think it would somehow affect me almost as much as the very person who was healed.

"All my life I've wanted to be in the healing ministry. Maybe I've never said it so clearly before or dared to dream that it would happen, but it's what I want. Now what do I do?"

And we prayed together asking God to show us.

Lindsay continued to encourage me and to ask the Lord about what He was doing in my life. She began to pray with me and I began to pray with her. We began to pray together about it every day. We started searching the Bible for every healing

Scripture we could find, especially in the four Gospels and the book of Acts...until we felt as if we saw Jesus rising up out of the pages of the Bible. We saw that *He's a healing Jesus.*

All my life I'd heard my dad talk about his experiences in the year before he started his healing ministry in 1947 — of coming to know Jesus as a healing Lord — but now we were experiencing it for ourselves. Lindsay and I got hold of Mark 11:24, "What things soever ye desire, when ye pray, believe that ye receive them, and ye shall have them," and a real desire came into my heart to see sick people healed. I began to have a different feeling...a much stronger feeling...than I'd ever had about the Oral Roberts Ministry I'd known all my life. I knew that my dad was getting older, and I didn't want to see this ministry die when Oral Roberts died someday.

I began to seek God for a healing ministry... and to do whatever I needed to do to move into it. I remember praying, "Lord, You said that when we pray we should believe that we receive 'whatsoever things we desire.' Now, Lord, Your Word is either true, or it's a lie...and I'm going to take You at Your Word. I want to have a healing ministry. I want to be a blessing to people. I want to be able to preach, teach, and pray for the sick *and to see results.* So in the name of Jesus, I ask You for a healing ministry, and by my faith I receive it and I believe it is now on the way."

As Lindsay and I prayed, we knew that we didn't have a healing ministry yet. But we believed it was on the way. For weeks and weeks around

our house we continued to claim Mark 11:24, and
if you'd been there you would have heard us saying
over and over again, "Thank You, Lord, for the
healing ministry that we believe is on the way."

Now you have to be careful with that Scripture.
Because some people think they can use it to say,
"Well, I just believe that I receive $2 million," and
God will rain it down from heaven in $20 bills. But
that's not how God works.

I'm talking about *your* desire being according
to the Bible, according to God's will in your life . . .
that it lines up with God's Word, not some crazy
thing or some pie-in-the-sky whim, but something
that makes sense. I believe that God makes sense.
And He expects *us* to use our common sense in life.

I knew that God was calling me into a healing
ministry of my own. He was the One who had put
the desire in my heart in the first place and He had
been dealing with me too much about it lately for
me to ignore it any longer. So I prayed and I waited
. . . and for a while nothing seemed to happen.

Until one night in Albuquerque, New Mexico.

From the moment I walked into the auditorium,
I knew something different was happening. When
my feet hit the platform and I began to preach,
the message I had prepared the night before completely vanished from my mind. God gave me a
new sermon that night and I preached it with an
authority in my voice like I'd never known before.

When I'd finished preaching, I then gave the
people an opportunity to stand and accept Jesus
Christ into their lives. That night about five hundred
people stood.

Then before I hardly knew what I was doing, I heard myself say, "If there's anybody here with arthritis, stand up. I want to pray for you to be healed."

I'd never spoken words like that before; I'd never learned those words anywhere. But to my amazement, three or four hundred people stood up, just waiting for me to pray for them. And I remember thinking to myself, *What have I done?* and *What if I fail?* Then clear as a bell I heard the Lord's voice speak in my spirit, *You've already done that. Besides, you're not going to heal the people. I am.*

And so I began to speak in the authority of the name of Jesus like I'd never known it was possible to speak before. "In the name of Jesus," I prayed, "I come against this arthritis. I rebuke you and command you to come out!"

And I looked up and saw people starting to move their shoulders that had been stiff earlier. When I came into the auditorium I had noticed a woman about 70 years of age sitting in the front row who was on an arthritic walker. But *now* I saw that her husband was waving the walker in his hand as she walked up and down on her own in front of the platform! Well, I could hardly believe my eyes!

I called to her, "Ma'am, what are you doing?"

"I'm walking," she called back.

And still almost overwhelmed by what was happening, I said, "Why are you walking?"

"I'm healed!" she cried. "Can't you see?"

"Yes, I can see. But, woman, I didn't touch you."

"*You* didn't have to touch me," she replied. "Jesus did."

With that the crowd burst into applause and into praise to the Lord for what had just happened.

I called out, "Is anybody hurting in your eyes, or have blindness, glaucoma . . . anything like that? Stand up if you do."

And I prayed again in Jesus' name. Far over to my left I heard a woman scream, "I can see! I can see!"

And I had one of the ORU Singers who traveled to my services with me to take his microphone and go over and talk to this young woman. "I've been blind in this eye for four years now," she said, "and when you spoke, the sight came back into my eyes. Praise God, I can see you now . . . I can even see the twinkle in your eye!"

Again, people almost went up through the roof of the auditorium. And I said to them, "Is anybody deaf . . . or have ear problems? Stand up so I can pray."

See, when the power of God came over me, I quit worrying about whether or not I would fail or what people would think of me. Lindsay says that when the anointing of God is on me, I become like another man.

And that man didn't know that it couldn't be done!

That man became like the bumblebee who doesn't know he's not supposed to be able to fly. They say it's scientifically impossible for a bumblebee to fly because its wingspan is too short for its body. But nobody's told the bumblebee, so he just keeps on flying!

And I just kept on praying! I rebuked the deafness in people's ears the way that Jesus rebuked it in the Bible.

A man stood up and shouted, "I've been deaf in this ear for ten years. Now I can hear!"

On and on it went the rest of the service that night. It occurred to me as I thought about the people who were healed that I never laid hands on any of them. My dad had always told me that when he prayed for the sick he felt the power of God up and down his right arm into his hand. But I'd felt that same kind of power rising up in my chest and coming out over my voice as I spoke the word of faith. And immediately my mind flashed to the story in Matthew 8 where Jesus encountered the Roman centurion whose servant was sick at home. When Jesus heard of his condition, He said to him, "I will come and heal your servant." But the centurion, recognizing Jesus' authority, replied, "Lord, You don't have to come to my home. For I also am a man under authority, having soldiers underneath me. And when I say to one man, 'Go,' he goes, and to another, 'Come,' he comes. You just speak the word, and I know my servant will be healed." (See Matthew 8:5-9.)

I learned that what I was feeling in my chest and coming up out of my mouth when I spoke was the anointing of the Holy Spirit to speak to the disease and to the sick person just as Jesus would have spoken to them. As time went on I also found that as I prayed for people, strange things would often happen in my body. When I would pray for someone who was deaf or hard of hearing, for instance, my ear might begin to snap and pop, like

when you're descending in an airplane. Or maybe
my knee or my shoulder would begin to crack and
pop. Even though I knew I was in good health and
there was nothing wrong with me, for a while I
thought maybe my body was falling apart!

But in time, I learned that's just the particular
way God deals with me in giving me a word of
knowledge — another of the nine gifts of the Spirit
in 1 Corinthians 12 — that someone's receiving a
healing. I know to speak that out ... because I
learned that when I don't, I start to stutter until
I do. Nothing else that comes out will make any
sense until I get into obedience and speak what
God is impressing me to speak.

You see, even though I sometimes feel foolish
speaking out what I feel God is impressing me to
say — like the night I prayed for that man's toe —
I've learned that it's not up to me to heal anyone.
I *can't* heal anyone; only God can heal. I'm just
the instrument God sometimes uses to give people
a word from Him so they can hold on with their
faith and receive the healing that God has for them.

When I walked off the auditorium platform in
Albuquerque that night in April 1980, I knew in
my heart that what I had prayed for, believed for,
and received by my faith was finally a reality in
my life.

Since that time the anointing of God on me to
preach the gospel and pray for the sick has grown
stronger and stronger. I've traveled across this
country and around the world conducting healing
crusades and seeing more miracles than I could
begin to tell you about. In one year alone I recently

had the privilege of leading more than half a million people to Christ and seeing thousands upon thousands receive miracles of healing in their bodies, emotions, finances, families, and in every area of their lives.

I believe God is just beginning to bring me into the fullness of what He has for my life and for my ministry. Since 1980 I have preached extensively in the United States as well as six foreign nations — Jamaica, Nigeria, Swaziland, South Africa, Norway, and Canada — some of them more than once, and God has shown me that in the coming years of my ministry He will open the doors for me to minister in 40 nations around the world. I believe that in many of those nations I will have the opportunity to minister to the heads of state, just as I did in Swaziland in 1984 where I was the first white man in the history of that tiny kingdom ever to lay hands on their queen and pray a healing prayer for her and for their country.

Friend, Richard Roberts is no one special when it comes to what God can do in a human life that is completely and totally sold out to Him. What's happened to me is not because I am great, but because the God I serve — THE GOD OF A SECOND CHANCE — is *great* . . . and His Son, Jesus Christ, lives inside me.

The only boast that I can make is one that Paul the apostle made to King Agrippa in Acts 26:19, "I was not disobedient unto the heavenly vision [that God gave me]." All I can say about Richard Roberts is that he's a man who is obedient to God. He's not a man without mistakes, without

faults and failures. But I know that Paul made
mistakes too. And look what God did for the world
through his life!

God has given me a SECOND CHANCE. It
began more than five years ago now. And let me
tell you, friend, I've finally gotten hold of God...
and just like the words to a song I often sing...

"I *won't* let go of His blessing,
I've fought too hard to believe,
I've lived through too many storms
To have what I have received.
I *won't* let go of His blessing,
I have a dream I still can see,
Regardless what may ever come my way,
I won't let go of His blessing me."*

What About You?

Will you make those words *your* song too? Will
you take hold of *all* God has for you? Will you put
the heavenly desires of your own heart before God
and ask Him to *give* them to you? I believe that
when you do, He'll answer you beyond anything
you can imagine today!

*Words/music by Mike Murdock; Win=Way
Productions, Inc./ ASCAP*

VII.

Our Miracle Baby, Jordan Lindsay

Our lives have not been without struggles since Lindsay and I married in 1980 and my healing ministry began later that year. As anyone who has been divorced can probably tell you, besides being emotionally devastated from the experience, often you are financially devastated as well.

But I believe that we have put our priorities into the right order for coping with those problems and with anything else that might come against us in the future. First, we are dedicated to God . . . and secondly, we are dedicated to each other.

Lindsay understands that my dedication to God, which includes the healing ministry, must be first in my life. My relationship with God and my calling are one. My wife and my family come after that. And therefore, because our priorities are in order, our marriage and our commitment to God fit like a hand in a glove.

Now that's not to say that everything is rosy every day of our lives. We continue to have disappointments and shattered dreams just like everyone else. Nowhere in the Bible does God tell

us that just because we're serving Him, we'll never
have problems. In fact, when you're serving God,
I believe the devil tries even harder to "devour"
you. That's where our ability to *trust* God becomes
all-important.

Jesus told His disciples, "In the world ye *shall*
have tribulation: but be of good cheer; I have over-
come the world" (John 16:33). Jesus clearly warned
that there would be times of struggle for us as
Christians. And then He promised us that if we
would turn to Him in those times, no matter how
deep the pain, He would not allow the struggles
to *destroy* us.

In the midst of our darkest personal tragedy,
Lindsay and I found God's Word to be true. On
January 17, 1984, Lindsay gave birth to our first
child ... a son ... Richard Oral Roberts. He lived
only 36 hours. No words can describe the pain we
felt ... the hurt, the disappointment, the anger at
the devil ... and the absolute trust that God required of us in that moment.

When Lindsay was 18 years old, she was told
by a physician that the chances of her conceiving
a child were very slim. After we married and began
trying to have children, we ran into that prediction
headlong. Lindsay did become pregnant, but she
miscarried before she was more than a few months
along. Then in 1982 she developed a very painful
cyst on her right ovary. After taking her over to
the City of Faith Health-Care Center, we learned
she'd have to have surgery to remove the cyst.
There was even the possibility, depending on how
large the cyst had grown, that she could lose one

ovary. We knew that the loss of an ovary would only lessen our chances of her ever becoming pregnant again.

That weekend my dad and I conducted one of our Faith and Healing Seminars on the Oral Roberts University campus. Lindsay came to every session of the seminar. She wanted to spend as much time as she could building up her faith and praying for other people's healings. The Bible says in James 5:16, "Pray ye one for another, that *ye* [the person doing the praying] may be healed." We believe very strongly in that Scripture on healing. I have seen many, many healings take place through this ministry when the person in need of healing begins to pray for someone else. Their prayers are a seed of faith they are planting to the Lord and God often multiplies that seed back to them in the form of their *own* healing. Many times we've seen both the person being prayed for *and* the person doing the praying healed!

Lindsay went out into our seminar crowd that weekend, praying for as many people as she could — in spite of her own pain. After the closing Sunday morning service we went over to the City of Faith to check Lindsay into the hospital for surgery on Monday. Before we checked her in, though, we prayed together. We believed that God could heal her *supernaturally* through prayer and the seeds of faith Lindsay had planted that weekend at our seminar. We also believed He could heal her *naturally* through the good work of the doctors and the surgery. Or He could heal her *through a combination of both*. We just wanted Lindsay healed...

and it did not matter how God chose to do the
healing.

The doctors again examined Lindsay and found
the cyst on her ovary still there. That night as
Lindsay read her Bible, she was drawn to the
promise of Jesus in Matthew 17:20 — "If ye have
faith as a grain of mustard seed, ye shall say unto
this mountain, Remove hence to yonder place; and
it shall remove; and nothing shall be impossible
unto you." A favorite song of mine — "Mountain,
You Gotta Move" — is based on that Scripture.
Lindsay could feel the cyst and she put her hand
over it and spoke: "Mountain, you be removed!"
And she went to sleep with her faith strong that
a miracle was on the way.

I returned to the hospital early the next morning
before Lindsay went into surgery so we could spend
a little time together and pray again. Then, not
too long after they'd taken Lindsay in for surgery,
I got a call from the doctor. He said, "Richard, we
made the incision on your wife and looked inside,
but I'm happy to tell you that what we'd seen
on the ultrasound machine and what we had felt
in our examination of her . . . is completely gone.
There is absolutely no evidence whatsoever of
the cyst!"

God had healed Lindsay through prayer even
before the surgeon's knife touched her and we were
very grateful for the miracle of God's healing power.
But because we had used wisdom in having the
surgery as we'd planned, God gave us a second
miracle that day!

As I continued talking to the doctor about

Lindsay, he told me that they *had* found something else. He said, "We found an infection in Lindsay's cervix that we might not have found had we not done the surgery. It's a low-grade infection that many women have, but most of them are able to tolerate it. In *young* women, many times it keeps them from being able to have children. Now we can treat that infection medically and ask the Lord to heal it."

Within a few days, Lindsay's infection had completely cleared up. We rejoiced together and thought that maybe *now* we could have a child. Lindsay did become pregnant again some months later...

But she miscarried again.

Then in 1983 Lindsay conceived and this time she carried the baby full term! We were ecstatic with joy as we made all the preparations necessary at home for our new baby.

On January 17, 1984, Richard Oral Roberts came into the world and we thought our hearts would burst with joy. He was a beautiful little boy... one that we had prayed for.

And, oh, how I wanted a son.

I have my two beautiful daughters, Christi and Juli, whom I love with all my heart and see as often as I can, but for years I had dreamed of one day also having a son. Richard Oral was the fulfillment of that dream.

Then within hours of his birth, our son became seriously ill. The doctors did everything they knew to do medically. Lindsay and I and many of our friends and family members prayed with all of our faith. My dad has had many experiences through the years of his ministry in praying for people who are seriously ill. He knows when the spirit of death is on someone . . . and he felt that spirit on our little boy. As we prayed and as Dad prayed, we felt the power of God in that room so strongly that I know that prayer was what held back the spirit of death for the 36 hours that little Richard Oral lived.

But something happened in that hospital intensive care unit that was simply beyond our control. Just 36 hours after his birth, our precious child went to heaven to be with the Lord.

How do you make it through something like that? Losing the son that you've dreamed of having . . . the child that never could have been conceived without a miracle of God?

As we stood over our baby's bed and wept, I heard myself saying through my tears, as Job said, "Though God slay me, yet will I trust in Him" (Job 13:15). And though I hurt like I'd never hurt before, I meant what I said.

Lindsay and I prayed together in the Spirit many times during the next days and weeks. We came to know the Comforter — the Holy Spirit of God — in a way that we'd never known Him before. In the midst of our deep grief and pain, we had the assurance in our hearts that we would one day see our baby again in heaven.

Shortly after Richard Oral's death, we were scheduled to go to Africa to conduct a month-long crusade . . . and even though we were still grieving over the loss of our child, we stuck by that commitment. God reminded me that I had a desire in my heart that was even greater than my desire to have a son. He reminded me that my *deepest* desire was to be an evangelist . . . to preach, to pray, and to see people healed. God told us to go to Africa . . . and that through our ministering to other people, He would heal our hurt. We obeyed God and during that African crusade we saw more people come to Christ and more people healed — mighty, *miraculous* healings like those in the Bible days — than in any other crusade we've ever conducted. The lame leaped . . . the blind saw . . . the deaf heard. One hundred thousand people stood to accept Jesus as their Savior and Lord. Lindsay and I had our faith renewed. Our hearts began to heal. We came home with a great determination in our spirits to see the new Childbirth Center completed at the City of Faith in Tulsa, Oklahoma.

Then . . . God gave us a SECOND CHANCE to have a child. Though the devil fought us and tried to make us believe that Lindsay and I would *never* be able to have another child, Lindsay became pregnant again. And on April 23, 1985, Jordan Lindsay Roberts was born — an 8-pound, 6-ounce, 21-inch-long beautiful baby girl.

By the way, little Jordan was born in the Childbirth Center at the City of Faith — the same Childbirth Center that was started after Richard Oral's death.

Already, Jordan has added such joy to our home! No, Lindsay and I have not forgotten about the loss of our son, and we never will. But we know he is with Jesus now, in heaven. And who knows, some day little Jordan just might have another brother or sister!

What About You?

Are you facing a situation in your life that man has told you is impossible to solve? Are you living with a broken heart that the devil has told you God can never heal? If you are, Lindsay and I know what you're going through. If we had believed the devil's lies that we could never have a child, or if we had believed that if we did have a child he would not live, then the devil would have had us gripped in fear for the rest of our lives. But we know that the God we serve is THE GOD OF A SECOND CHANCE. So we tried again. And we rebuked the devil's attempts to paralyze us with fear or with guilt.

God has made a promise to us in His Word that as we serve Him with all our heart, He *will* restore what the worm (or the devil) has destroyed. (See Joel 2:25.) Job, in the book of Job, is a perfect example of someone who had lost everything he owned and everything he held dear. Yet, Job determined to trust the Lord and to serve Him no matter what happened and no matter what other people said. In the end, God restored to Job all that he had lost, and more besides. The Bible says that God restored *twice* as much to him as he had before. (See Job 42:10.)

Through the birth of our daughter, Jordan Lindsay, God has restored to us many times over what the devil had stolen from us in the death of our son. As we've purposed in our hearts to serve God all our days and to praise Him in all circumstances, we've seen Him literally turn our lives around.

Give God *your* loss, your impossible situations, your heart broken from sorrow, and watch Him turn your life around for good. HE'S THE GOD OF A SECOND CHANCE.

Now I Want to Pray Especially for You

Friend, I believe that at this very moment, God has a SECOND CHANCE for YOU in every area of your life. No matter what your problems seem to look like...no matter how big that giant of despair and discouragement, fear, poverty, disease, strife in relationships, or some demonic oppression seems to be. Why? Because God is bigger than your problems. He's bigger than any need you're facing in your life. And no matter *what* you're going through God can turn it around...and give you that SECOND CHANCE you need.

God *cares* about you. I know He cares because He's put His care for you in me. He's concerned about you and about meeting every need that you have — spiritually, physically, financially, emotionally, and in your family.

Let's pray:

"O Lord, I come to You today, not in my name or in my strength, but in the mighty incomparable name of Jesus Christ of Nazareth, the only Son of God who died for our sins and who carried the burden of our guilt ...that we as human beings might not have to carry it. I thank You, Lord, that You *are* bigger than any problem we face...and that

You came to bring us, not judgment and condemnation, but love, forgiveness, and a SECOND CHANCE in those areas of our life where we've failed."

And, friend, I reach my hand out to *you* now. My hands are just human hands, but the moment you release your faith and believe, they can represent the healing hands of Jesus extended toward you and the places where you're hurting in your life.

"In the name of Jesus, I come against the pain and the failure of your past. I come against the guilt and the torment...the thoughts of suicide that you may have been feeling because of what people say. I pray for you to be healed in your memories...in your emotions...beginning this moment, and to cast your cares upon Jesus...for He cares for you.

"I come against that physical condition in your body...that's telling you you'll never make it another day. In the name of Jesus, I rebuke that disease...that pain...and I command it to set you free. May you be healed in your body and know what it is to have the strength and the joy of the Lord coursing through your veins again.

"For that financial problem you're facing... I say, 'Devil, take your hands off God's property. I command you to loose their money and let it go.' Friend, as you plant your seeds of faith to God and look to Him only as your Source, may you experience financial blessing like you've never known it before.

"And I pray for that situation, that problem, that is tearing your family apart. In the name of Jesus, I come against the strife and the confusion in your home. And I command it to be gone forever. Be healed in your family and in your relationships with all your loved ones . . . and may you know the power of God in a dynamic new way in your home.

"Friend, I believe these things for you and I receive them in Jesus' name . . . knowing that the God I serve is truly the GOD OF A SECOND CHANCE for *you*.

Amen and amen."

Why a Live Daily Television Program?

Since September of 1984, the *RICHARD ROBERTS* show has been on the air Monday through Friday. It's an opportunity that God has given me to go into people's homes five days a week *live* with the SECOND-CHANCE message of the gospel. Through this hour-long program of music, ministry, and personal prayer, we're helping millions of people know that no matter what problem or situation they're facing in life, God can turn that problem around for their good. He'll give them a SECOND CHANCE at life just like He's given to me.

Someone asked me recently, "Why are you doing a live daily TV show?" I'd like to give you the same answer I gave them. It's the story of a man in Chicago named Jerry Wood.

When I first received a letter from Jerry, he had been in and out of prison several times and had been mainlining heroin. He told me that one Sunday morning he was in desperate need of a "fix." He had called his drug dealer to try and find some "stuff." But as Jerry was getting ready to go out his front door to make a score, he stopped. For some reason, he turned on his TV and sat down to watch it. As he did, our Sunday morning tele-

vision program came on the screen. I happened to
be preaching and ministering that day, and right
at that moment I was getting ready to pray. Just
as I'd done many times before, I asked the people
who were watching the program and who needed
to be healed to put their hands on the TV set as a
point of contact to release their faith. Miraculously,
Jerry did just that.

The moment I prayed, he felt something different
on the inside of him. As I prayed, Jerry prayed
too and gave his heart to Jesus Christ. Suddenly
the desire for heroin left him! He went back to bed
and slept several hours, got up and took a shower,
ate breakfast . . . still with no desire for heroin.

Several months later, Jerry wrote me and told
me the story of what had happened to him through
watching our Sunday morning television program.
He told me how his entire life had changed. He
told me how God had helped him get a new job
and a new apartment. His neighbors, who had once
feared Jerry, now trusted him enough to allow him
to be the manager of the apartment complex where
he lived! His family, who had turned against him
because of his drug habit and his stealing to get
money for the habit, now had been restored to a
good relationship with him. And the best part of
all — he was now ministering out on the streets to
people who were just like he'd once been.

God gave Jerry Wood a SECOND CHANCE at
life.

As I read Jerry's letters I wondered what would
have happened if Jerry had turned on his TV set
on any other day of the week but Sunday. I knew

that the more often we were on the air with the
message of the gospel, the more people like Jerry
Wood we'd be able to reach; I had been feeling that
in my spirit for some time. God had been dealing
with me that it was time for me to make a live
daily television program and to reach into the
homes of millions of people with desperate needs.
But Jerry Wood was the catalyst that God used
to begin the *RICHARD ROBERTS* show in September 1984.

Since my daily program began, we have been
flooded with phone calls from people watching who
are in desperate need of a SECOND CHANCE in
their life. In order to handle all the calls we receive,
we've had to expand the Abundant Life Prayer
Group from 7 prayer partners to 60. I've often
said that the more testimonies I read over the air,
the more testimonies we receive. Every day through
the outreach of the *RICHARD ROBERTS* show, I
receive reports from people who are discovering,
just like Jerry Wood did and like Richard Roberts
did, that

HE'S THE GOD OF A SECOND CHANCE.

I believe that's a message you'll want to help
me take around the world. You can do it by becoming a Partner with me and by helping me expand
our daily television ministry outreach. Together,
we can give the hope of a SECOND CHANCE to
every person who needs one.

Help Me Reach More People With the Message of a SECOND CHANCE

I want to give you the greatest opportunity of your life to be a Partner with me in taking the message that HE'S THE GOD OF A SECOND CHANCE to people around the world. You can do that by planting a seed in this ministry of just $20 a month and becoming a Partner with me in expanding our live daily TV program. You'll be helping me reach more and more people every day who desperately need to know God and His healing power . . . and to hear Jesus' message of a SECOND CHANCE.

When you become a Partner with me, I want to send you:

- a beautiful *lapel pin* to remind you that no matter what you've done in your life God *can* TURN IT AROUND and give you a SECOND CHANCE.

- a TURN-IT-AROUND *plaque* to place on your kitchen table, TV, or somewhere else in your home where you will see it frequently.

- a new *album* of some of the most popular songs from my daily program recorded *live*.

Just fill out the coupon on the next page and return it to: **Richard Roberts, Tulsa, Oklahoma, 74171**

Richard, I want to become a Partner with you. Here is my Seed-Faith pledge of . . .

☐ $20 a month   ☐ Other $_____

☐ Send me my lapel pin, plaque, and record album, *RICHARD ROBERTS LIVE*.

☐ Please send me a cassette tape instead of an album.

Name_____
                                                    683

Address_____

City_____

State_____ ZIP_____

**This FREE Booklet
Will Help Get Your
NEW LIFE in Christ
Off to a Good Start**

If you have just accepted Jesus Christ as your Lord and Savior while reading this book, I want to give you something that I believe can help get your new life in Christ off to a good start...and help keep it on track for years to come. In this 28-page booklet, *HOW TO LIVE YOUR NEW LIFE,* I talk to you about the importance of reading your Bible regularly, going to church, praying, and learning to make God your Source of total supply.

Read this booklet and then ask the Lord to show you through His Word even more ways in which you can develop a strong, secure relationship with Him.

Fill out the coupon below and mail it to:
Richard Roberts, Tulsa, Oklahoma 74171

Richard, I accepted Jesus Christ into my heart as a result of reading this book.
Please send me my FREE copy of your booklet, *HOW TO LIVE YOUR NEW LIFE.*

Name_____
684

Address_____

City_____

State_____ ZIP_____

If you
need prayer . . .
ANYTIME
DAY OR NIGHT
Dial
918 • 495-7777

The Prayer Tower, Oral Roberts University, Tulsa, Oklahoma

City of Faith Health-Care Center
Tulsa, Oklahoma

FOR APPOINTMENTS
CALL . . .
918 • 493-8181